Favorite CLASSICAL Melodies

TENOR SAX

Arranged and Recorded by David Pearl
("Brandenburg Concerto No. 5, First Movement" arranged and recorded by Donald Sosin)

Cherry Lane Music Company
Director of Publications/Project Supervisor: Mark Phillips

ISBN: 978-1-60378-413-9

Visit our website at www.cherrylaneprint.com

CONTENTS

AVE MARIA

By Charles Gounod and Johann Sebastian Bach

TENOR SAX

Moderately slow

BRANDENBURG CONCERTO NO. 5, FIRST MOVEMENT

By Johann Sebastian Bach

TENOR SAX

CARO MIO BEN

TRACK 3

TENOR SAX

By Giuseppe Giordani

CLAIR DE LUNE

TENOR SAX

By Claude Debussy

Slowly

FUNERAL MARCH OF A MARIONETTE

TENOR SAX

by Charles Gounod

Moderately fast, in 2

9

GYMNOPÉDIE NO. 1

TENOR SAX

By Erik Satie

HALLELUJAH CHORUS

from *Messiah*

TENOR SAX

By George Frideric Handel

HUNGARIAN DANCE NO. 5

TENOR SAX

By Johannes Brahms

MINUET
(from String Quintet in E Major)

By Luigi Boccherini

TENOR SAX

Moderately

PIANO SONATA NO. 14 "MOONLIGHT"

First Movement

TENOR SAX

By Ludwig van Beethoven

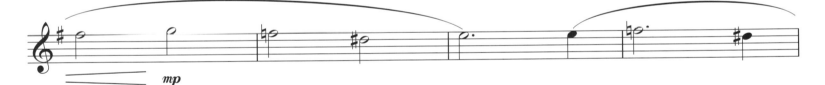

SYMPHONY NO. 5

First Movement

TENOR SAX

By Ludwig van Beethoven

WILLIAM TELL OVERTURE

TENOR SAX

By Gioacchino Rossini

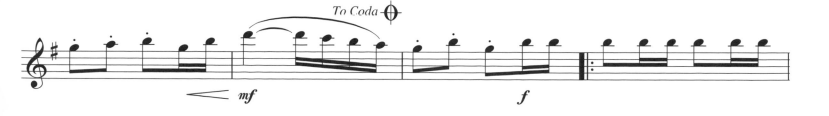

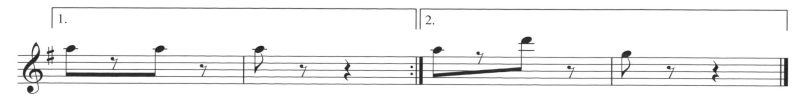

POMP AND CIRCUMSTANCE

TENOR SAX

By Edward Elgar

Moderately